W9-AOZ-776

EXPLORING THE STATES

Arizona

THE GRAND CANYON STATE

by Pat Ryan

BLASTOFF!
5
READERS

BELLWETHER MEDIA • MINNEAPOLIS, MN

Note to Librarians, Teachers, and Parents:

Blastoff! Readers are carefully developed by literacy experts and combine standards-based content with developmentally appropriate text.

Level 1 provides the most support through repetition of high-frequency words, light text, predictable sentence patterns, and strong visual support.

Level 2 offers early readers a bit more challenge through varied simple sentences, increased text load, and less repetition of high-frequency words.

Level 3 advances early-fluent readers toward fluency through increased text and concept load, less reliance on visuals, longer sentences, and more literary language.

Level 4 builds reading stamina by providing more text per page, increased use of punctuation, greater variation in sentence patterns, and increasingly challenging vocabulary.

Level 5 encourages children to move from "learning to read" to "reading to learn" by providing even more text, varied writing styles, and less familiar topics.

Whichever book is right for your reader, Blastoff! Readers are the perfect books to build confidence and encourage a love of reading that will last a lifetime!

This edition first published in 2014 by Bellwether Media, Inc.

No part of this publication may be reproduced in whole or in part without written permission of the publisher. For information regarding permission, write to Bellwether Media, Inc., Attention: Permissions Department, 5357 Penn Avenue South, Minneapolis, MN 55419.

Library of Congress Cataloging-in-Publication Data

Ryan, Patrick, 1948-
Arizona / by Pat Ryan.
     pages cm. – (Blastoff! readers. Exploring the states)
Includes bibliographical references and index.
Summary: "Developed by literacy experts for students in grades three through seven, this book introduces young readers to the geography and culture of Arizona"–Provided by publisher.
ISBN 978-1-62617-002-5 (hardcover : alk. paper)
1. Arizona–Juvenile literature. I. Title.
F811.3.R93 2014
979.1–dc23

2013002376

Table of Contents

Where Is Arizona?

Arizona is a rectangular state in the southwestern United States. It shares its southern border with Mexico. California and Nevada lie across the Colorado River to the west. Arizona's northern neighbor is Utah. New Mexico lies to the east. The state also touches corners with Colorado in the northeast.

Phoenix is the state capital. The city stands along the Salt River in southern Arizona. It is also the state's largest city. Several other major cities are clustered around Phoenix.

California

N
W E
S

Nevada

Did you know?

Northeastern Arizona touches Utah, Colorado, and New Mexico at a place called Four Corners. This is the only place in the United States where four states meet.

Grand Canyon
National Park

Utah

Colorado

Colorado River

New
Mexico

Arizona

Glendale

Phoenix ★● Mesa

Chandler

● Tucson

Mexico

5

History

The first people may have arrived in Arizona over 25,000 years ago. More than one-fourth of the state's land still belongs to **Native** Americans. In 1540, explorer Francisco Vásquez de Coronado claimed Arizona for Spain. Mexico took control of the state in 1821. In 1848, most of Arizona became part of the United States. Arizona was granted statehood in 1912.

Mexican-American War

Arizona Timeline!

1540: Francisco Vásquez de Coronado explores Arizona. He claims the land for Spain.

1821: Mexico takes control of Arizona.

1848: The United States wins the Mexican-American War. Mexico gives up land that includes most of Arizona.

1854: Copper is first mined in Ajo, Arizona.

1863: The Arizona Territory is created.

1912: Arizona becomes the forty-eighth state.

1948: Arizona's Native Americans are granted the right to vote.

1981: Arizonan Sandra Day O'Connor becomes the first female Supreme Court Justice of the United States.

2010: Arizona passes a strict law meant to reduce the number of Mexicans who live there illegally.

Francisco Vásquez de Coronado

Native Americans

Sandra Day O'Connor

The Land

Arizona has three main regions. The Colorado **Plateau** covers the northern part of the state. **Mesas** and mountains break up this flat land. **Canyons** are carved by the Colorado River. This region is known for its beautiful shades of purple, red, and orange. South of the plateau, the land drops into a rugged area of mountains and pine forests.

The **Basin** and Range region includes much of southern Arizona. Mountain ranges cut through the gently sloping desert landscape. The Sonoran Desert lies in the southwest. Summers in Arizona are hot, dry, and full of sunshine. Winters vary from mild in the southwest to cold in the northeast.

fun fact

About 50,000 years ago, a large chunk of rock from space hit Arizona. It made a hole about 4,180 feet (1,274 meters) wide and 570 feet (174 meters) deep!

8

Did you know?

Saguaro cactuses are found only in the Sonoran Desert. These giant plants can grow more than 50 feet (15 meters) tall and weigh up to 20,000 pounds (9,072 kilograms)!

Arizona's Climate

average °F

spring
Low: 56°
High: 85°

summer
Low: 78°
High: 104°

fall
Low: 61°
High: 87°

winter
Low: 43°
High: 68°

The Grand Canyon

Did you know?

A trip into the Grand Canyon is like a trip through time. Its colorful stripes are different layers of rock that have built up over two billion years!

Almost 5 million people visit northwestern Arizona's Grand Canyon every year. They marvel at its size and beauty. The canyon is 277 miles (446 kilometers) long and up to 18 miles (29 kilometers) wide. It is one of the largest canyons in the world. The mighty Colorado River cuts deep through layers of multicolored rock. It leaves behind rocky peaks and **buttes** that stretch through the **horizon**.

The Grand Canyon began to form around 6 million years ago. The Colorado River slowly **eroded** the rock along its course. Its waters still shape this natural wonder today. The shifting light of the Arizona sun highlights the changing nature of the canyon.

Wildlife

Arizona's mountains, forests, and deserts provide shelter for many animals. Large cats are common in forested areas throughout the state. Mountain lions climb Arizona's rocky peaks. They hunt prey such as mule deer and elk. Bobcats sometimes wander close to people's homes. The state's forests also hide black bears. Bighorn sheep can be seen scrambling up canyon walls.

The deserts are home to tortoises and pig-like animals called javelinas. **Venomous** scorpions and Gila monsters scurry across the sand. Falcons, hawks, and other birds of prey circle overhead.

bighorn sheep

javelina

Gila monster

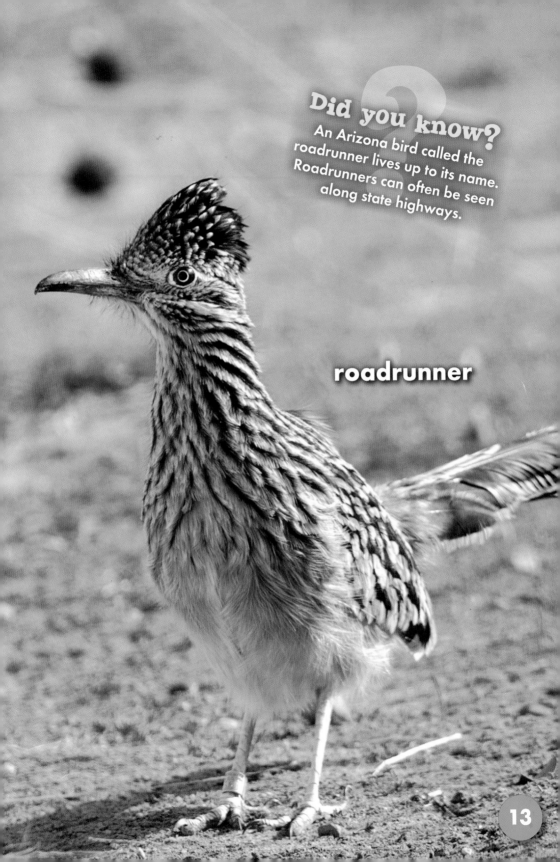

Did you know?
An Arizona bird called the roadrunner lives up to its name. Roadrunners can often be seen along state highways.

roadrunner

Landmarks

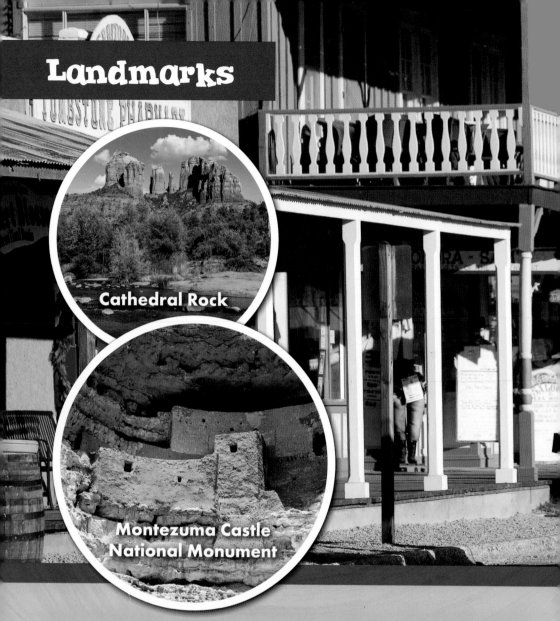

Cathedral Rock

Montezuma Castle
National Monument

Arizona's desert landscapes draw millions of **tourists** each year. Many stop near Sedona to see Cathedral Rock and other beautiful red rock formations. The Painted Desert in northeastern Arizona is named for its striking bands of color. In the east, Petrified Forest National Park contains a wide range of plant and animal **fossils**.

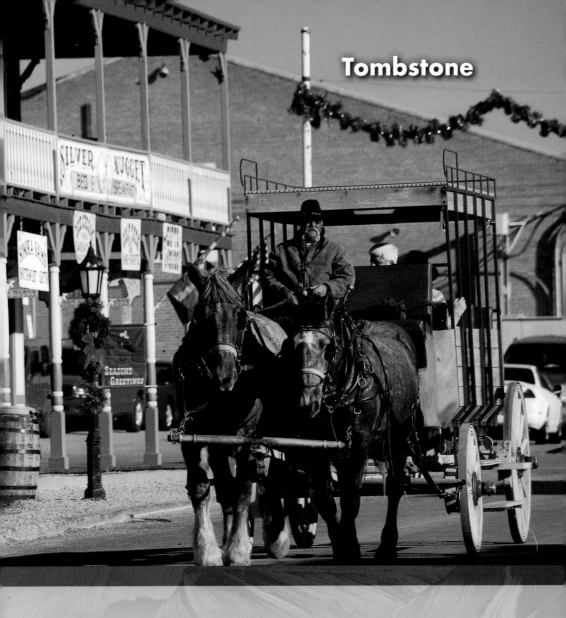

The Wild West can still be seen in Tombstone. This southeastern Arizona town once attracted **outlaws** such as Wyatt Earp and Doc Holliday. Today, their famous gunfight comes to life in a **reenactment** at the O.K. Corral. The Montezuma Castle National Monument near Camp Verde takes visitors back almost 1,000 years. It features homes that Native Americans built into a cliff.

Phoenix

The city of Phoenix gets its name from a **mythological** bird. The phoenix rises from its own ashes after dying in a fire. Arizona's capital rose from the **ruins** of a community that died out in the 1400s. Today Phoenix thrives in the hot desert. More than 4 million people live in and around the city.

Phoenix lies in the Salt River Valley, where mountains tower over the skyline. One of the buildings downtown is Symphony Hall. Here, audiences enjoy ballets and Phoenix Symphony concerts. Many tourists come to sunny Phoenix in winter. Golfing and hiking are popular activities. The city's Chase Field is home to the Arizona Diamondbacks baseball team.

Symphony Hall

Chase Field

Working

Did you know?

Arizona is a center for Native American crafts. Many artists make and sell rugs, silver jewelry, baskets, and other handmade items.

Mining and farming have always been important jobs in Arizona. Workers dig for copper, silver, and gold. Coal and oil are found in northeastern Arizona. The state's **irrigated** farmland is good for growing lettuce, cotton, and **citrus fruits**. Farmers also raise cattle and sheep on large ranches.

Factory workers make high-tech products such as airplanes, spacecraft, and electronics. They also produce chemicals and metals. Many Arizonans have **service jobs** in government offices, hotels, and restaurants. The state relies on tourists and **retired** people for much of its income.

irrigation

Where People Work in Arizona

manufacturing
5%

farming and
natural resources
2%

government
13%

services
80%

Playing

Arizonans can hit the snowy slopes and sunny golf courses all in one day. The mountains near Flagstaff are covered in snow during winter. They are perfect for downhill and cross-country skiing. In the south, visitors can enjoy summertime activities throughout the year. Golf, baseball, and softball are popular sports. Boating and waterskiing are common on Arizona's lakes.

The Arizona Trail offers more than 800 miles (1,287 kilometers) of beautiful hikes. It stretches from the Mexico border to the Utah state line. Hikers and mountain bikers also take to the mountains. Arizona's highest point, Humphreys Peak, allows them to climb up to 12,633 feet (3,850 meters).

golf

mountain biking

Arizona
Diamondbacks

Fry Bread

Ingredients:

1 cup flour

1 teaspoon baking powder

1/8 teaspoon salt

1/3 cup warm water

Oil for frying

Directions:

1. Mix flour, baking powder, and salt.

2. Sprinkle in water until dough holds together. Cover and let stand for 30 minutes.

3. Divide dough in two. Flatten each into a 6-inch circle.

4. Heat 1 inch of oil to 375°F in a pan. Fry bread on each side until golden brown. Drain on paper towels.

5. Serve with taco toppings for a meal, or drizzle honey on top for dessert.

tacos

salsa

The mix of cultures in Arizona provides a variety of **traditional** foods. Native American and Mexican influences are especially strong. Fry bread is a Native American **staple**. This fried dough is often topped with beans, ground beef, and other taco fixings. It can also be served as a dessert with ice cream on top.

Tacos, burritos, and other Mexican dishes are made with tortillas. Salsas made with hot chili peppers add spice to these and other Arizona foods. Some types of **cactuses** are used in salsas and barbecue sauces. Barbecued beef is cooked over local mesquite wood.

**World Championships
Hoop Dance Contest**

Many festivals in Arizona honor the state's Wild West history. Cowgirls and cowboys saddle up for **rodeos** and horse races throughout the year. Prescott Frontier Days in July is said to be the world's oldest rodeo. Along with bull riding and calf roping, crowds enjoy a large parade and fireworks.

Window Rock hosts the Navajo Nation Fair. It is one of the world's largest Native American gatherings. The Navajo people celebrate and share their culture with dancing, rodeos, and the crowning of Miss Navajo. The dazzling World Championship Hoop Dance Contest takes place in Phoenix. Native people from the U.S. and Canada dance with as many as 50 hoops.

Cinco de Mayo

! fun fact

The Mexican holiday of Cinco de Mayo is widely celebrated in Arizona. People gather on May 5 to feast on Mexican food and enjoy music and dancing.

Native Americans in Arizona

Arizona has one of the biggest populations of Native Americans in the country. The Navajo are the largest tribe in Arizona. They live among the colorful rock formations in the northeast. They are proud to speak the Navajo language and follow their own religion. The Hopi live on and around three mesas within the Navajo Nation territory. They are known for their skill in creating pottery, baskets, carved dolls, and other crafts.

The second largest **reservation** in Arizona belongs to the Tohono O'odham. They live in the Arizona desert and speak the O'odham language. Several other tribes also thrive throughout the state. Their ancient cultures and beautiful lands make Arizona a special place.

fun fact !

A group of Navajo men called "code talkers" became heroes in World War II. They used their native language to create a secret code that no non-Navajo could break.

Fast Facts About Arizona

Arizona's Flag

The state flag of Arizona features a copper star on a field of blue. It represents the state's abundance of the metal resource. The star shines rays of yellow and red, the colors of Spain and the Arizona sunset. The stripes stand for the original thirteen colonies. The flag was adopted in 1917.

State Flower
saguaro cactus blossom

State Nicknames:	The Grand Canyon State The Copper State
State Motto:	*Ditat Deus*; "God Enriches"
Year of Statehood:	1912
Capital City:	Phoenix
Other Major Cities:	Tucson, Mesa, Chandler, Glendale
Population:	6,392,017 (2010)
Area:	113,991 square miles (295,235 square kilometers); Arizona is the 6th largest state.
Major Industries:	mining, farming, manufacturing, tourism, services
Natural Resources:	copper, gold, silver, coal, oil
State Government:	60 representatives; 30 senators
Federal Government:	9 representatives; 2 senators
Electoral Votes:	11

State Animal
ringtail

State Bird
cactus wren

Glossary

basin—an area of land that is lower than the surrounding land

buttes—narrow hills with steep sides and flat tops

cactuses—plants with spines instead of leaves; most cactuses are found in dry climates.

canyons—narrow river valleys with steep, tall sides

citrus fruits—fruits with thick skins and pulpy insides

eroded—slowly wore away with water or wind

fossils—remains of plants and animals from the past that are preserved in rock

horizon—the line where the earth seems to meet the sky

irrigated—watered using a source other than rainfall

mesas—wide hills with steep sides and flat tops

mythological—relating to old stories or beliefs of a group of people

native—originally from a specific place

outlaws—people who are wanted for breaking the law

plateau—an area of flat, raised land

reenactment—the performance of a historic event

reservation—an area of land the government has set aside for Native Americans

retired—no longer working

rodeos—events where people compete at tasks such as bull riding and calf roping; cowboys once completed these tasks as part of their daily work.

ruins—the physical remains of a human-made structure

service jobs—jobs that perform tasks for people or businesses

staple—a product that is widely and regularly used

tourists—people who travel to visit another place

traditional—relating to a custom, idea, or belief handed down from one generation to the next

venomous—producing a poisonous substance called venom

To Learn More

AT THE LIBRARY

Standard, Carole K. *Arizona*. New York, N.Y.:
Children's Press, 2009.

Yasuda, Anita. *Explore Native American Cultures!*
White River Junction, Vt.: Nomad Press, 2013.

Zuehlke, Jeffrey. *The Grand Canyon*. Minneapolis,
Minn.: Lerner Publications Co., 2010.

ON THE WEB

Learning more about Arizona
is as easy as 1, 2, 3.

1. Go to www.factsurfer.com.

2. Enter "Arizona" into the search box.

3. Click the "Surf" button and you will see a list of
   related Web sites.

With factsurfer.com, finding more information is just
a click away.

Index

The images in this book are reproduced through the courtesy of: Alexey Stiop, front cover (bottom); North Wind Picture Archives/ Alamy, p. 6; Traveler1116, p. 7 (left); Katrina Brown, p. 7 (middle); (Collection)/ Prints & Photographs Division/ Library of Congress, p. 7 (right); Zack Frank, p. 8 (small); Jo Ann Snover, pp. 8-9; Josemaria Toscano, pp. 10-11; Howard Sandler, p. 12 (top); Fotomicar, p. 12 (middle); Minden Pictures/ SuperStock, p. 12 (bottom); ElementalImaging, pp. 12-13; Keneva Photography, p. 14 (top); David Byron Keener, p. 14 (bottom); Age Fotostock/ SuperStock, pp. 14-15; Fotosearch RM/ Age Fotostock, p. 16 (top); AP Photo/ Ross D. Franklin/ Associated Press, pp. 16 (bottom), 24-25; Tim Roberts Photography, pp. 16-17; Megapress/ Alamy, p. 18; Federico Rostagno, p. 19; Brocreative, p. 20 (top); Jorg Hackemann, p. 20 (bottom); Keith Charles/ Icon SMI CHX/ Newscom, pp. 20-21; Lokibaho, p. 22; Joshua Resnick, p. 23 (top); Brent Hofacker, p. 23 (bottom); Mexican American Dance Troupe/ Getty Images, p. 25 (small); Saul Loeb/ AFP/ Getty Images/ Newscom, p. 26 (small); Ray Manley/ SuperStock, pp. 26-27; Pakmor, p. 28 (top); Jim David, p. 28 (bottom); Martha Marks, p. 29 (left); DLILLC/ Corbis/ Glow Images, p. 29 (right).